MY FIRST DINOSAUR BOOK

DANIEL FROST

TYRANNOSAURUS

Pronounced ty-ran-o-sore-us

Let's begin with the fiercest dinosaur of all—the Tyrannosaurus rex. With sharp teeth and killer claws, they are known as "king of the dinosaurs."

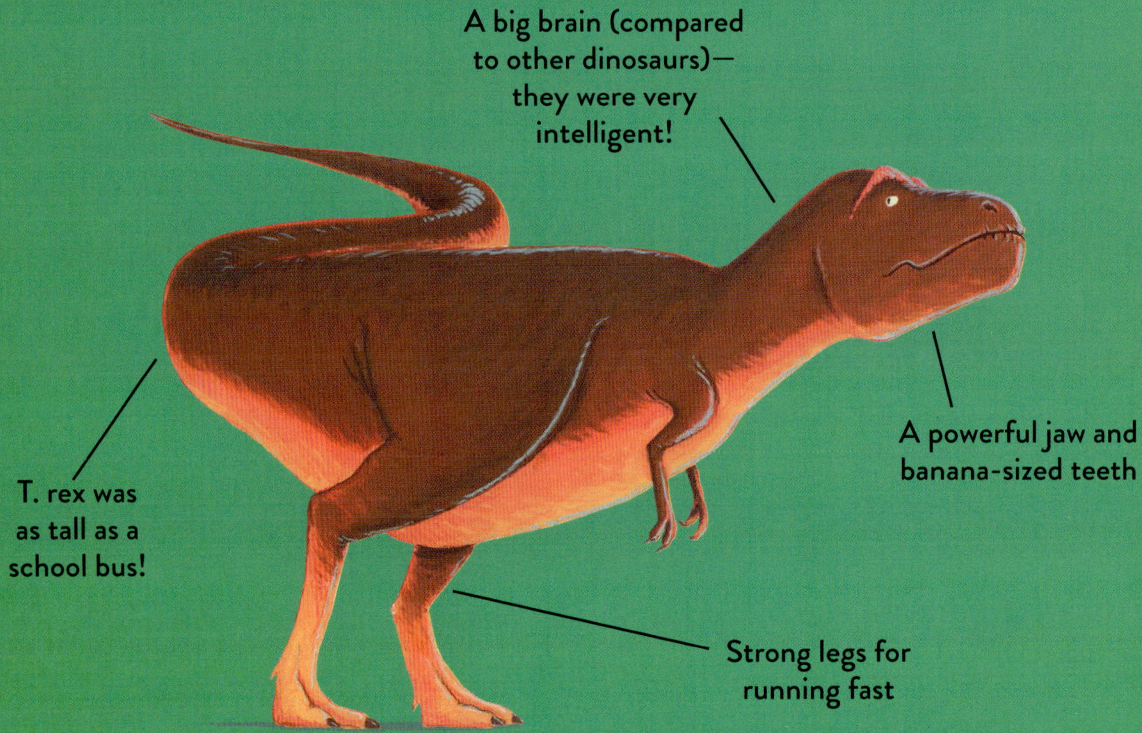

TRICERATOPS

Pronounced try-serr-uh-tops

Did you know that Triceratops means "three-horned face"? You can see why! These powerful creatures were similar to modern-day rhinoceros.

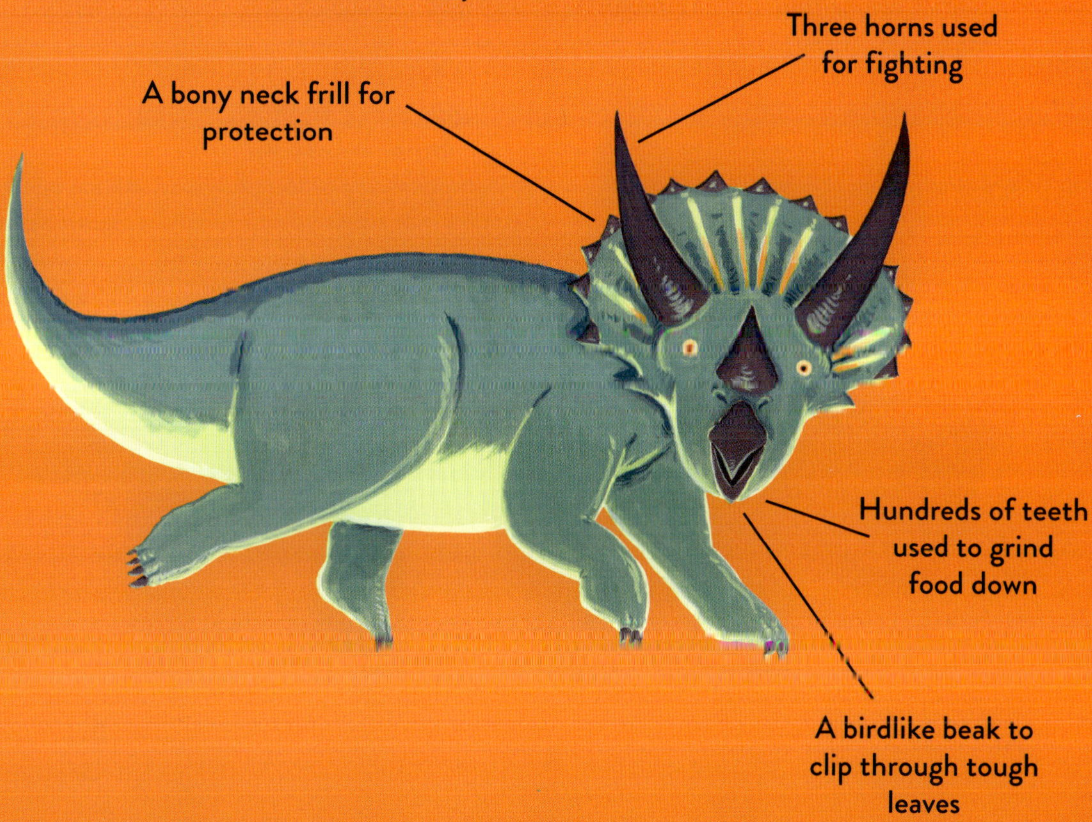

SPINOSAURUS

Pronounced spin-oh-sore-us

The Spinosaurus may have been even BIGGER and SCARIER than the Tyrannosaurus rex. In fact, they were the biggest meat-eating dinosaur of all time—bigger than a large elephant!

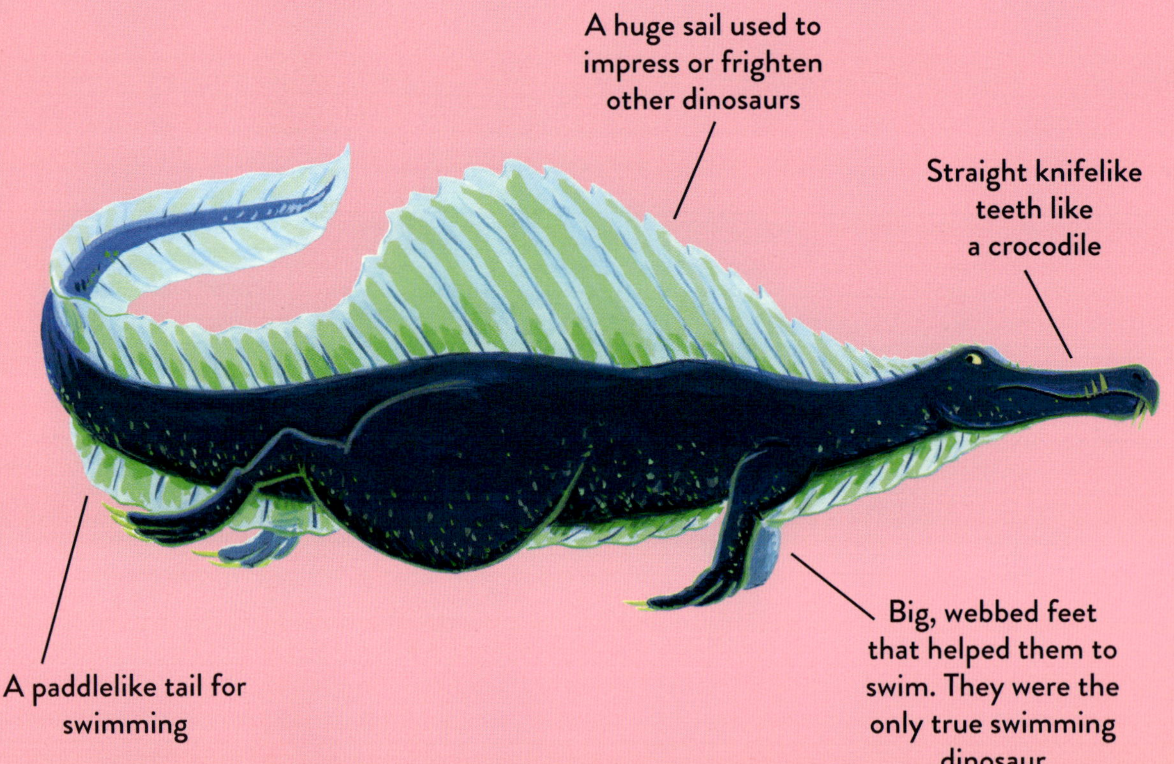

IGUANODON

Pronounced i-gwaa-no-don

Scientists learned that dinosaurs were reptiles because of Iguanodon teeth. They are very similar to iguana teeth. Iguanodon actually means "iguana tooth."

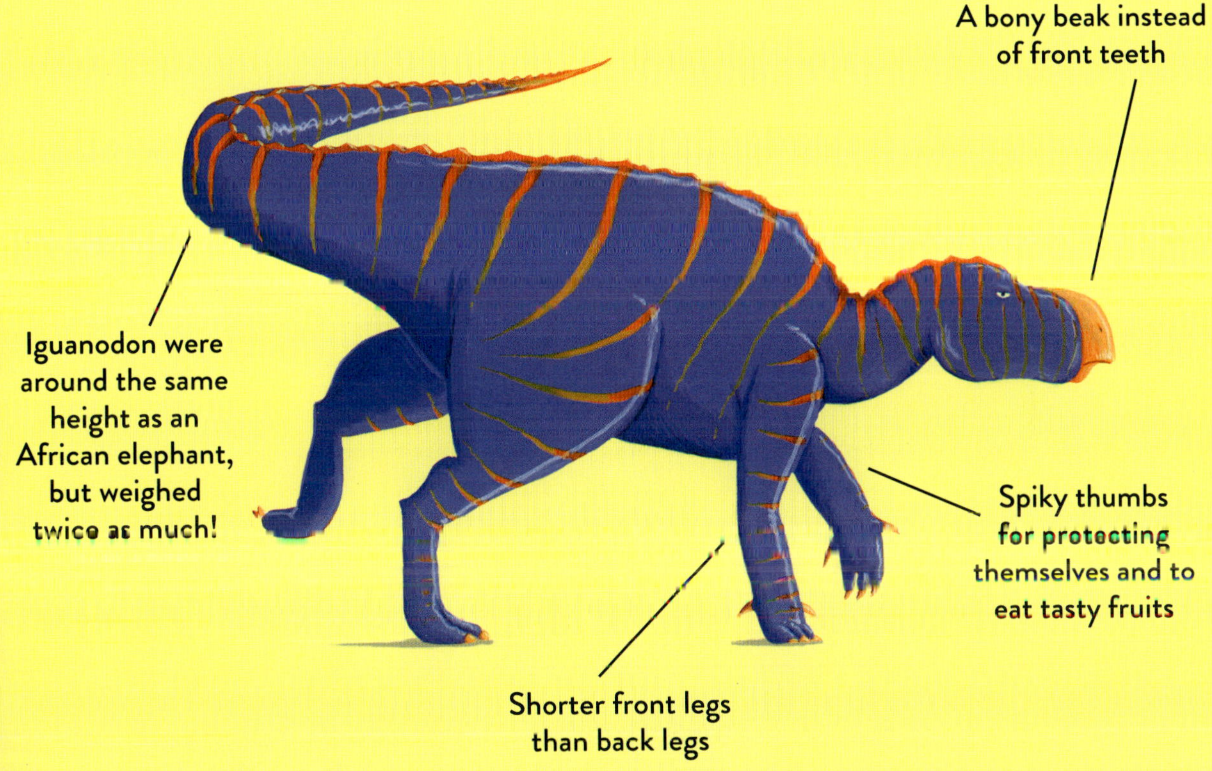

ANKYLOSAURUS

Pronounced an-kee-lo-sore-us

Ankylosaurus are known for their impressive armor. They even had armor in their eyelids! This kept them safe from bigger dinosaurs, like the T. rex.

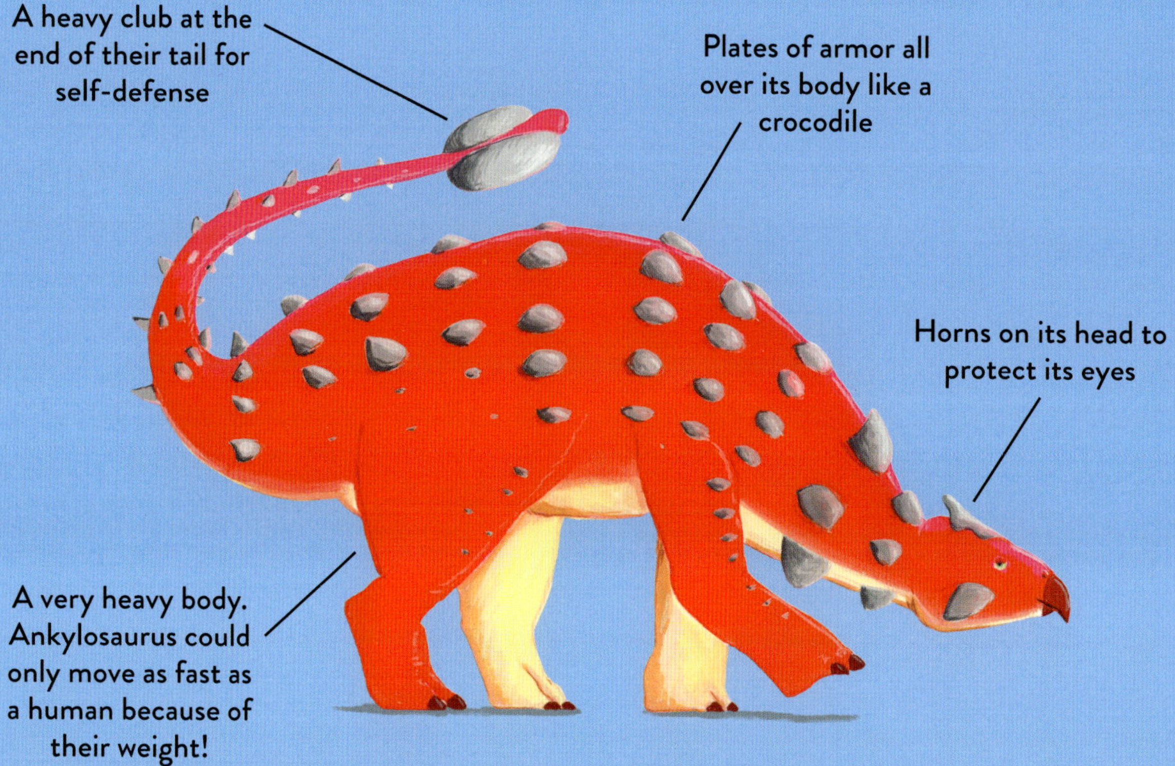

DEINONYCHUS

Pronounced die-non-e-cus

Deinonychus were quick and strong. Despite their small size, they were one of the fiercest predators. Deinonychus means "terrible claw."

COMPSOGNATHUS

Pronounced comp-sog-nath-us

Compsognathus were one of the smallest dinosaurs, around the same size as a chicken! Though don't be fooled—these small creatures used their sharp teeth to catch prey and often worked together to hunt bigger dinosaurs!

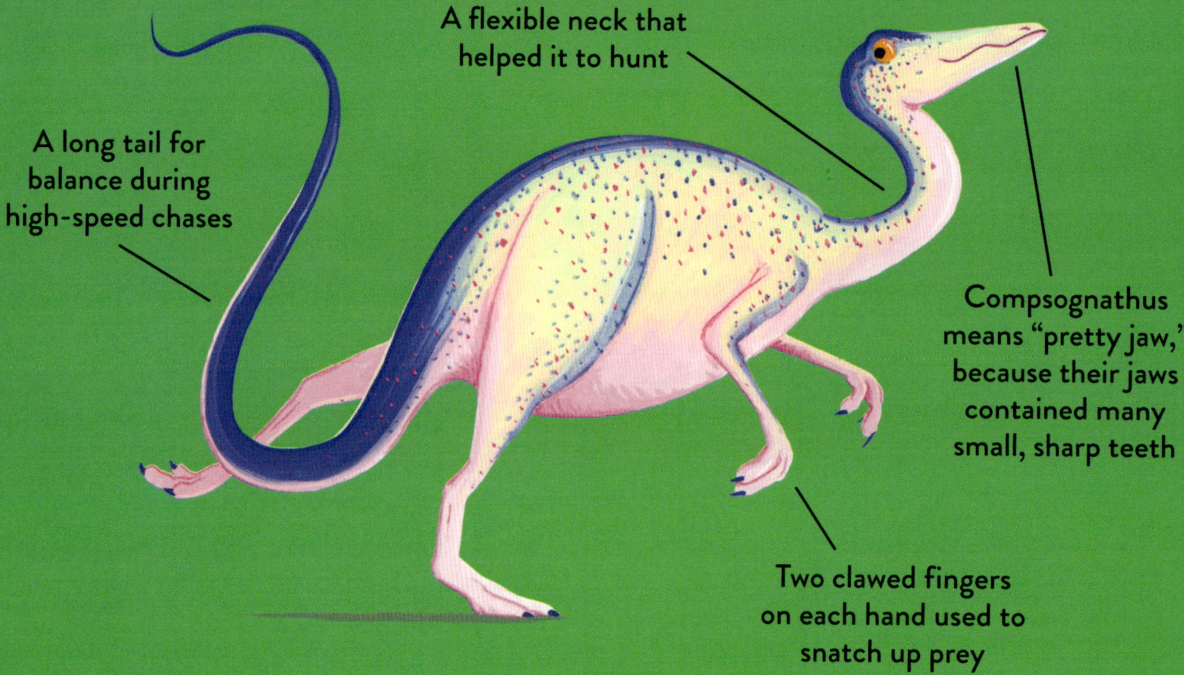

DIPLODOCUS

Pronounced dip-low-dock-us

These peaceful, plant-eating dinosaurs were the gentle giants of the Jurassic world. They lived in herds and spent their days chomping on leaves from high up in the trees.

STEGOSAURUS

Pronounced steg-o-sore-us

Though they look fierce, Stegosaurus were large, slow-moving plant-eaters. Also, with a brain the size of a walnut, they likely weren't very intelligent either!

VELOCIRAPTOR

Pronounced vuh-loss-uh-rap-ter

Velociraptor means "quick thief." These cunning creatures often sneaked around, looking for other dinosaur's eggs and food to snitch!

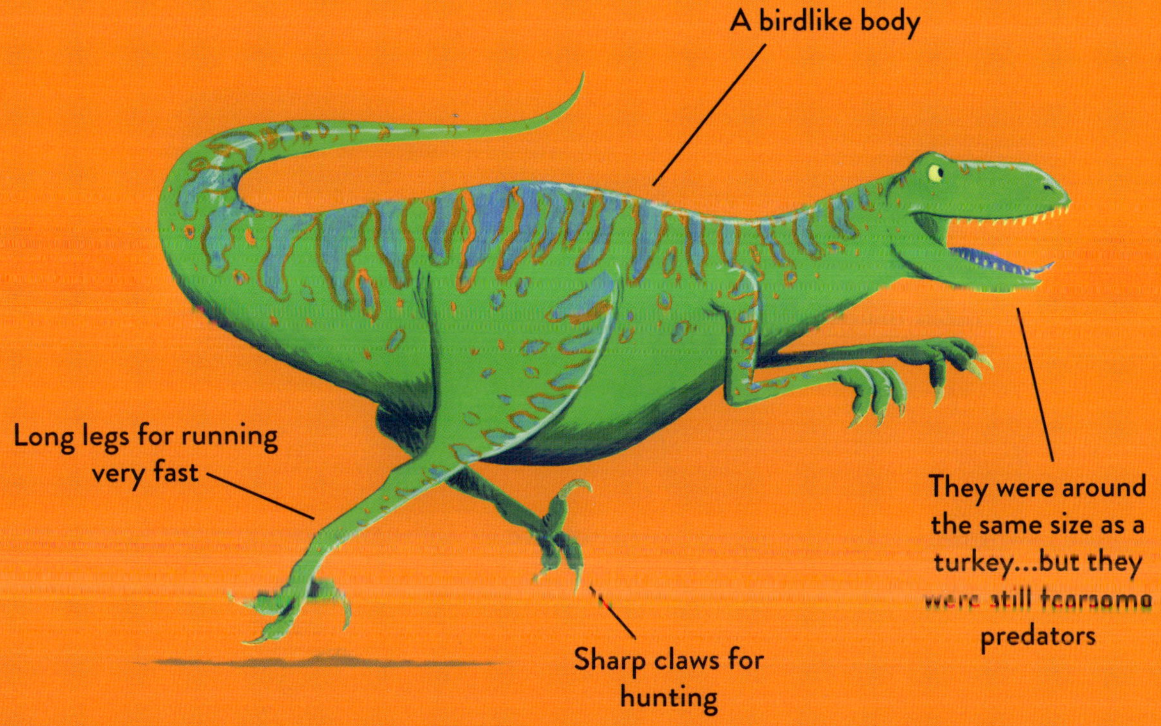

PARASAUROLOPHUS

Pronounced pa-ra-sore-ol-lo-fuss

These duck-billed dinosaurs are famous for their head crests, but they also had a special talent. They could sing...kind of!

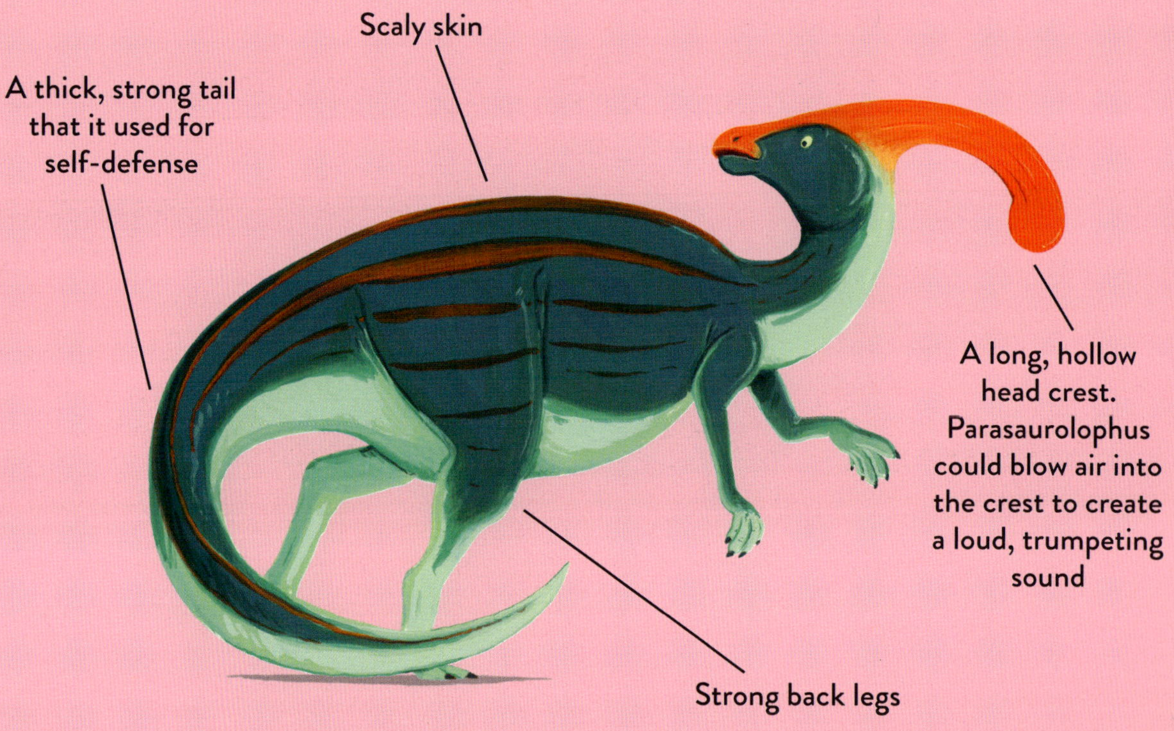

LAMBEOSAURUS

Pronounced lam-bee-o-sore-us

Like Parasaurolophus, Lambeosaurus had impressive head crests. We don't know what exactly they were for, but many believe they helped the dinosaurs to communicate.

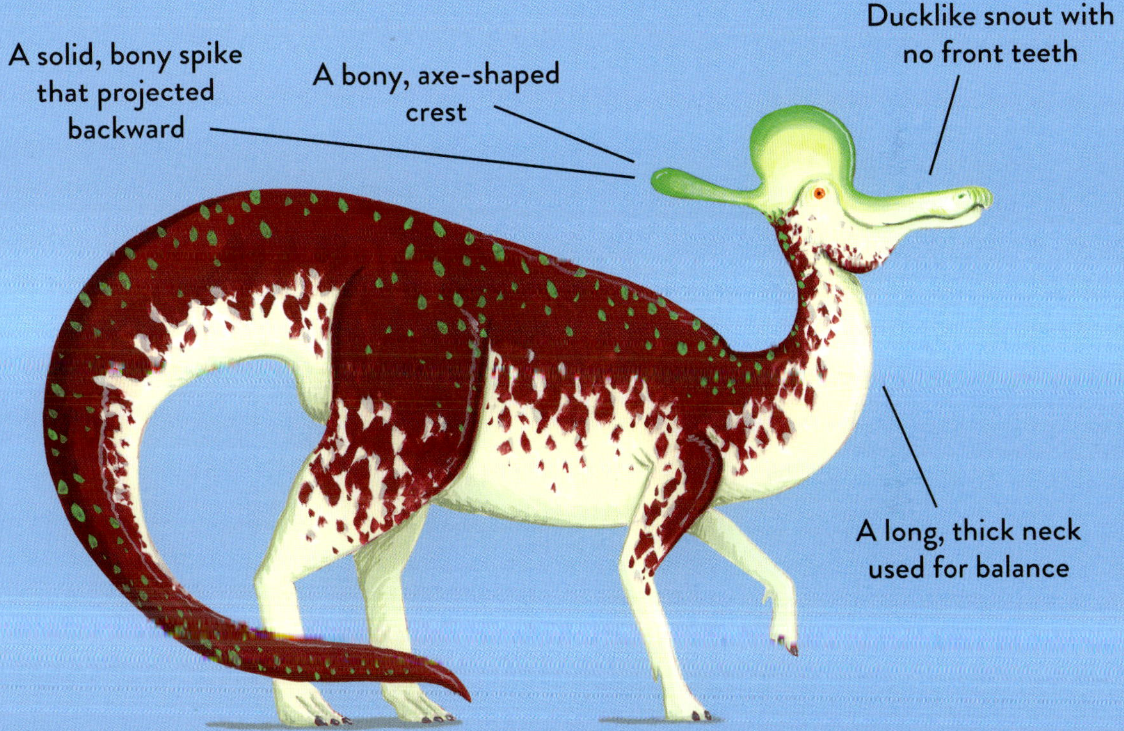

POLACANTHUS

Pronounced pol-a-can-thus

Polacanthus means "many spines" because of the spikes covering its back, shoulders, and tail. This was great protection against bigger dinosaurs as nothing could bite down on a Polacanthus without being stabbed by their spikes.

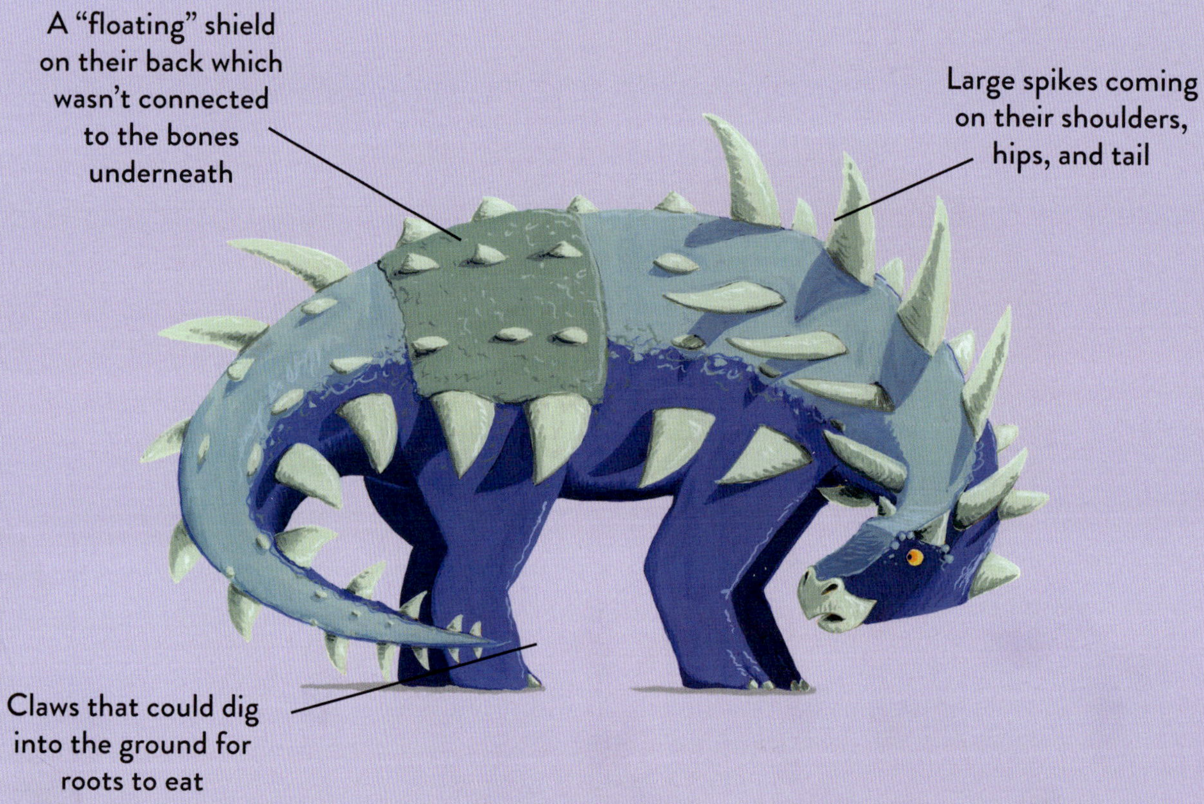

ARCHAEOPTERYX

Pronounced ar-kee-op-tuh-riks

Archaeopteryx are often referred to as the first known bird. These pigeon-sized dinosaurs taught us that birds descended from dinosaurs!

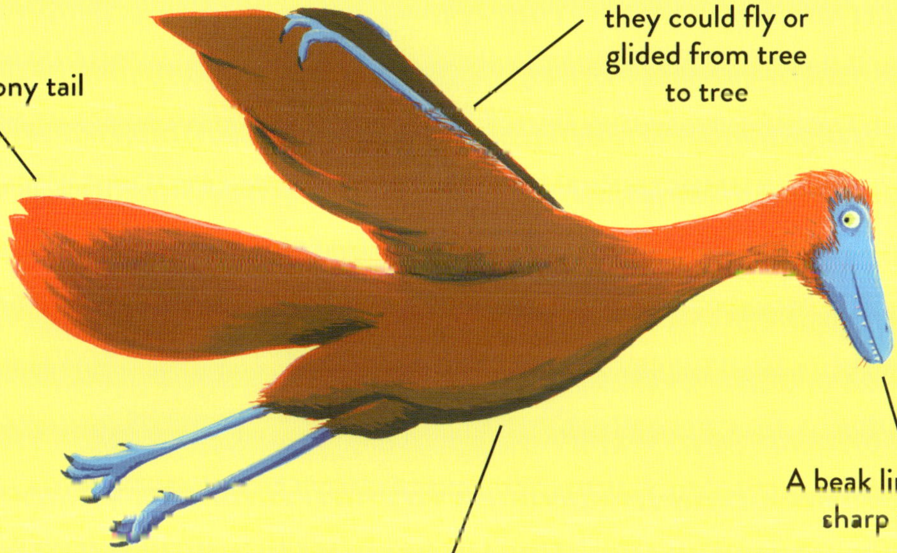

DILOPHOSAURUS

Pronounced di-la-fa-sore-us

Dilophosaurus are known for the distinctive frills shaping their face. The name means “two-crested lizard.”

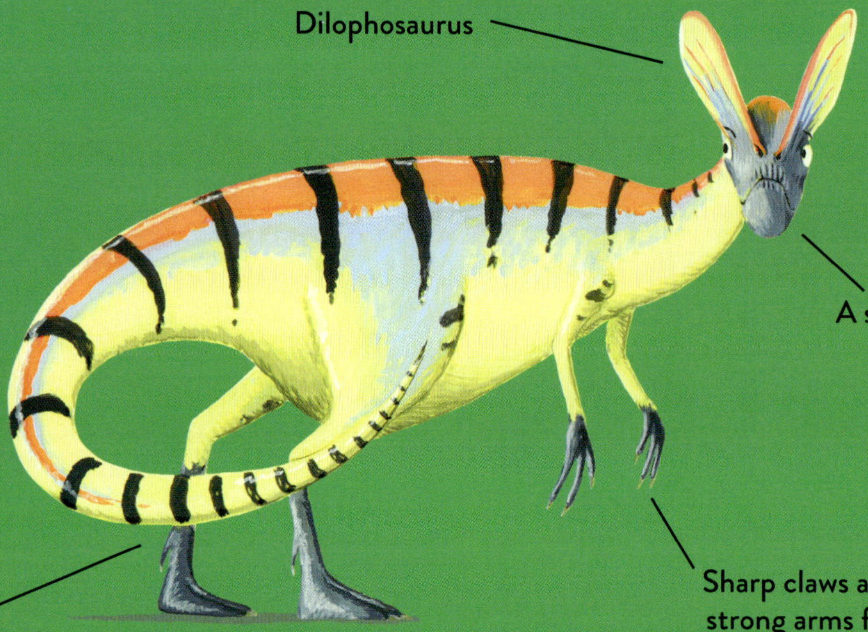

LETHOSAURUS

Pronounced leth-o-sore-us

We don't know much about Lethosaurus as only a few bones have been found. We only have a partial jaw and three teeth!

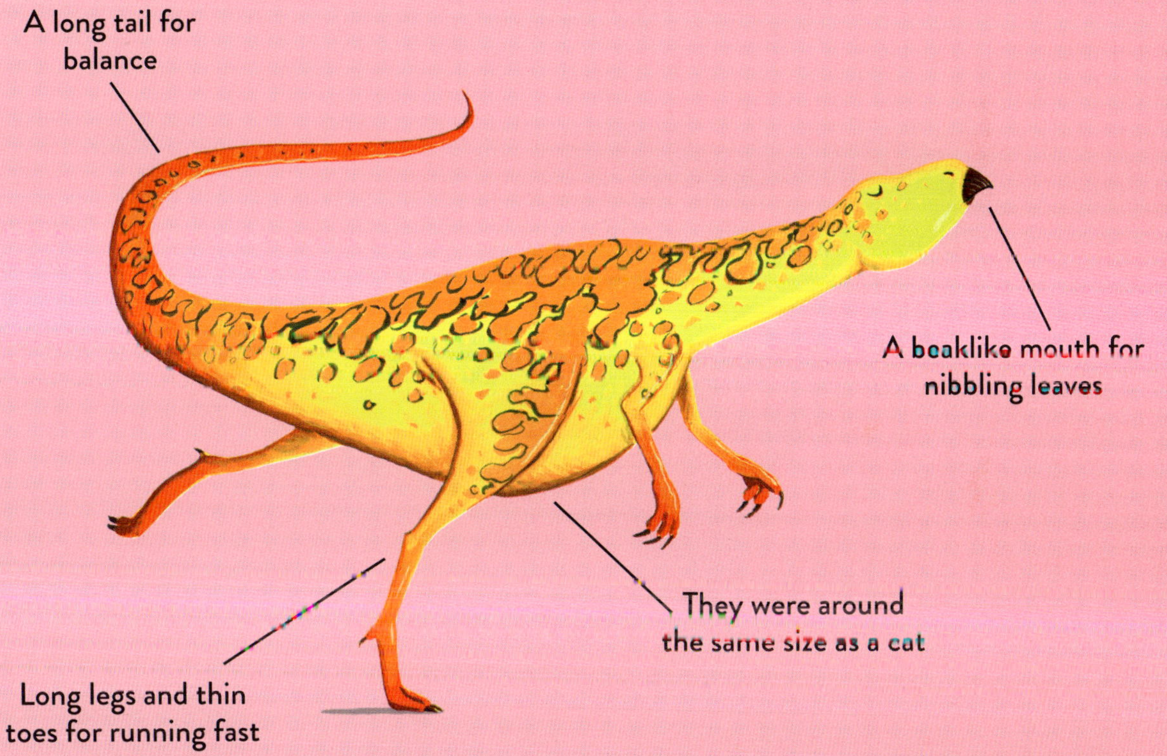

GORGOSAURUS

Pronounced gor-goh-sore-us

Gorgosaurus had 60 sharp, jagged teeth in its mouth, which it used to crack through bones. Eek!

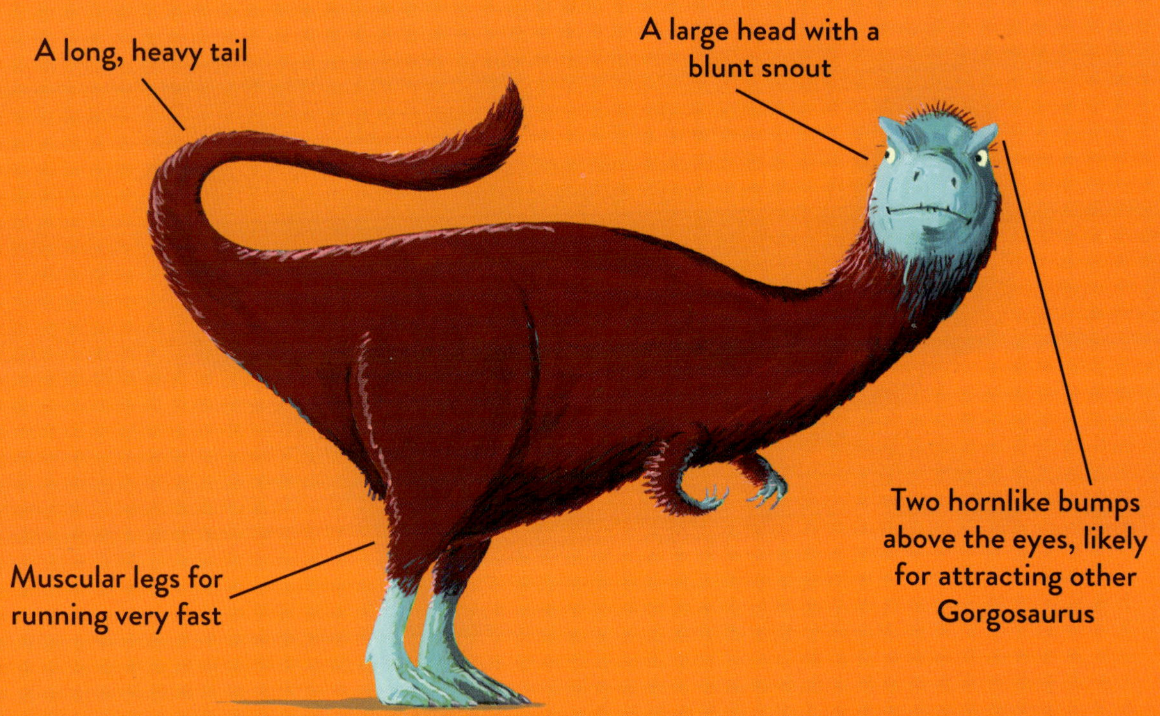

LEAELLYNASAURA

Pronounced lee-ell-in-a-sore-a

Leaellynasaura lived in what is now Australia when it was very cold and they had long, dark winters with very little daylight.

MICRORAPTOR

Pronounced mike-ro-rap-tor

Meaning "small thief," these tiny dinosaurs are known for being the littlest known dinosaur…for now!

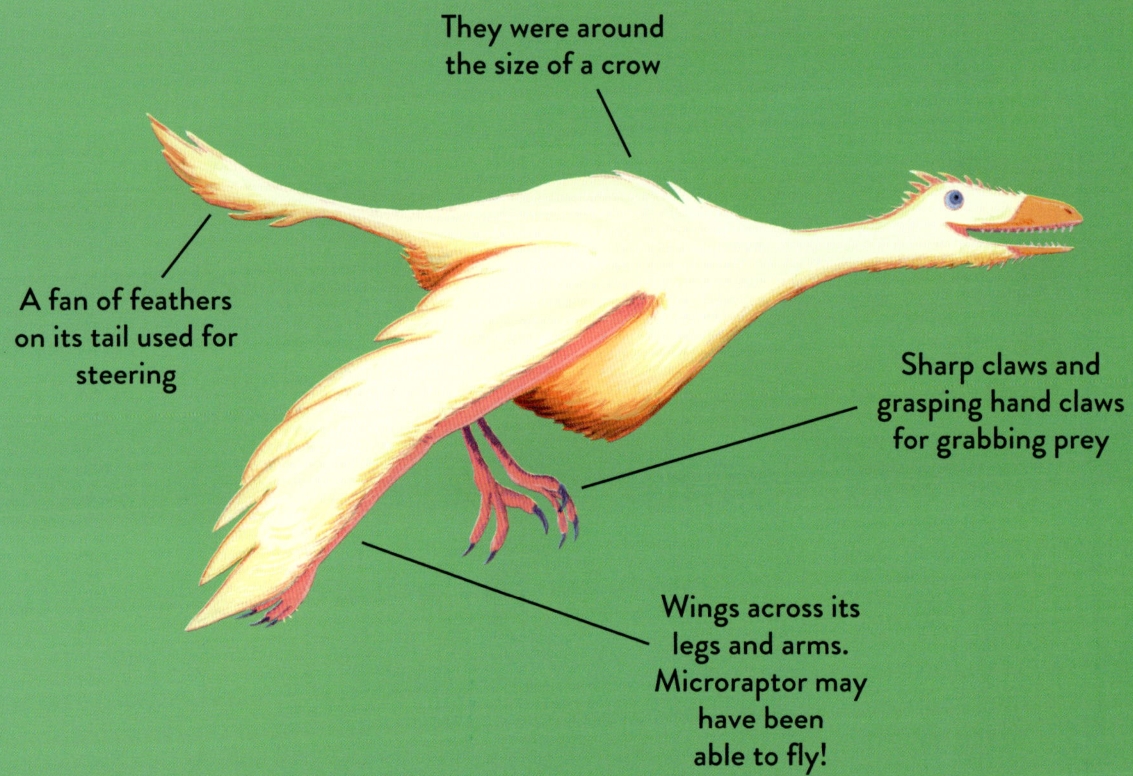

ORNITHOMIMUS

Pronounced or-nuh-tho-me-muss

Ornithomimus were small, birdlike dinosaurs. Their name means "bird mimic" because they look very similar to ostriches.

RINCHENIA

Pronounced rin-chen-e-uh

We don't know a lot about these mysterious dinosaurs as we have only found one, but we think that they are like Oviraptors!

SINOSAUROPTERYX

Pronounced sine-oh-sore-op-ter-iks

Sinosauropteryx were small, meat-eating dinosaurs. They roamed the savannas of what is now northern China.

THERIZINOSAURUS

Pronounced ther-uh-zy-no-sore-us

With long claws, bright feathers, and a round belly, Therizinosaurus are one of the strangest-looking creatures of all time.

EDMONTOSAURUS

Pronounced ed-mon-tuh-sore-us

These duck-billed, plant-eating dinosaurs could weigh as much as an African elephant. They were one of the biggest known dinosaurs!

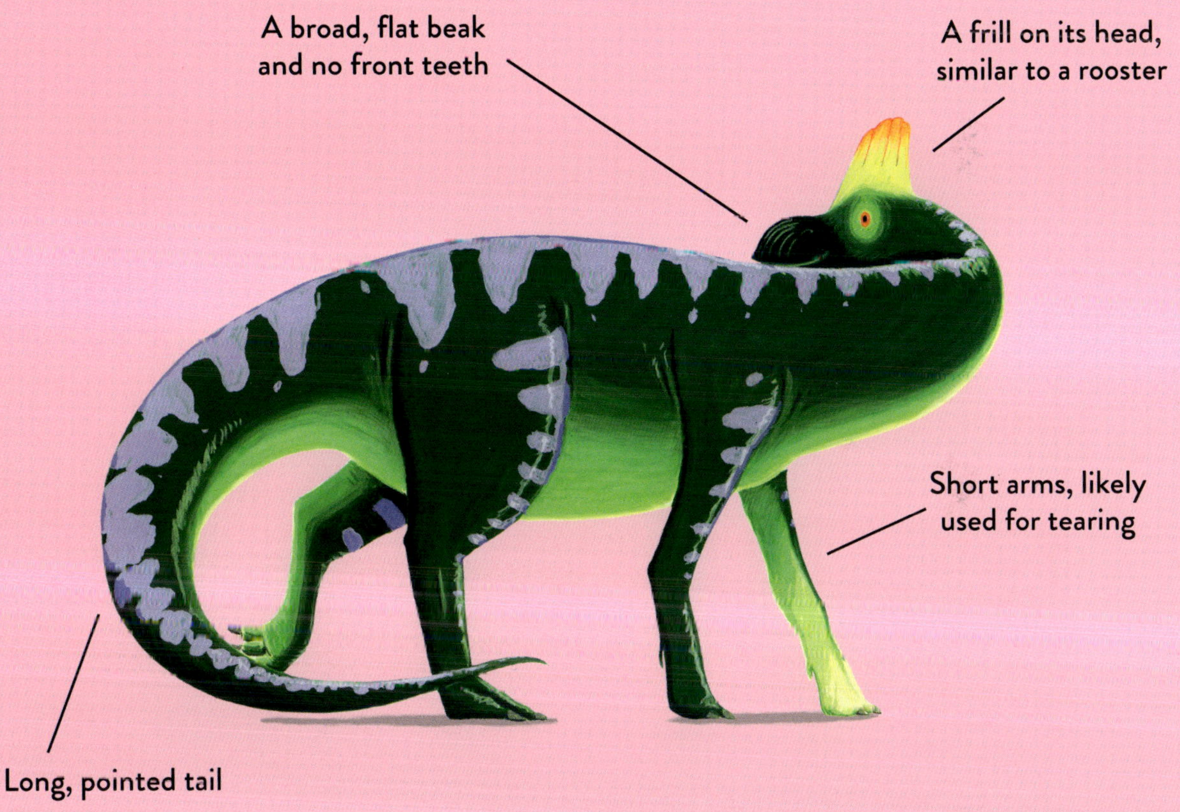

DINO DICTIONARY

ARMOR—a covering that protects the body

CREST—a raised point on the head of an animal

NECK FRILL—a bony border around the head of a dinosaur

HERD—a large group of animals that live together

JURASSIC—a period of history marked by the presence of dinosaurs and the first appearance of birds

PREDATOR—an animal that hunts other animals for food

PREY—an animal that is caught and killed by another animal for food

LAURENCE KING

First published in the United States in 2025 by Laurence King

ISBN: 978-1-5102-3171-9

10 9 8 7 6 5 4 3 2 1

Printed and bound in Dubai

MIX
Paper | Supporting responsible forestry
FSC® C104740
FSC www.fsc.org

Laurence King
An imprint of
Hachette Children's Group
Part of Hodder and Stoughton Limited
Carmelite House
50 Victoria Embankment
London EC4Y 0DZ

An Hachette UK Company
www.hachette.co.uk
www.hachettechildrens.co.uk
www.laurenceking.com